RELENTLESS EXECUTION

Everyday find time to do
Something good for yourself!
Yolanda

YOLANDA SPEARMAN

Foreword by Marlena Macrae

I would like to take a moment to thank everyone who believed in me. I especially want to call out my husband, Mark, my content editor and fact-checker. We shared many laughs over how I chose to write out some of my memories. To Marlena and Vicki, thanks for being the first two people to listen to me read the book and offer your advice and encouragement. Thank you, Marlin, because you know more than anyone how long this dream has lived inside me, and you have been there every step of the way—watching and waiting for this day with me. Thanks to Jocelyn and Marlena, my editors, for pulling more out of me than I thought possible and making this book better than I dreamed. Thanks to everyone who allowed me to share snippets of your story. Special thanks to God, who particularly inspired me to write this book. Thanks to everyone reading this book because you inspire me to write more.

Table of Contents

Foreword

by Marlena Macrae

Relentless Execution inspired me to dust off my dream book and get to work, making those dreams come true. It reminded me that I still have goals to check off my list. It motivated me to move forward with **Relentless Execution.** Here's how.

I am a creative person, which made going to graduate school to pursue an MBA a bit of a challenge. I had thought about a few different avenues my life could take to fulfill my dreams. Many of my goals were entrepreneurial, and I knew that going to business school would give me the tools I needed to succeed in my pursuits—whether creative, entrepreneurial, financial, or some combination of the three. Business school wasn't the most fun idea of all of those floating around in my head. I didn't go to bed at night dreaming about applied statistics, supply chain management, and Gantt charts. Still, it was a practical choice that would give me the tools to manage and monetize my fun in the future. For me, that was appealing.

Knowing that I live in a country where money buys freedom and opportunity, I needed to understand how to earn that degree and use it. Besides, I needed to learn how to be scrupulous and strategic, plan, save, barter, negotiate, and enjoy. Those are things that I consider essential practices for most Americans.

I played professional basketball abroad when I fractured my foot during the very last game of the season. I planned to return for another season, but limited mobility gave me time and allowed me to think about staying in the United States and working on aspects of my life beyond playing sports. I'd been an athlete all my life, and other than some recurring back issues, this was my first significant injury. In the past, I was called *graceful* on the court; but trust me, there was neither grace nor elegance in my ability to walk on crutches, and those handy knee scooters were not a thing at the time. As a result, I spent a lot of time sitting with my foot up, practicing RICE (Rest, Ice, Compression, Elevation), healing, thinking, and planning my future in my mind. After my foot healed and I was back in the States, I got a job working for a sports marketing company. One evening after work, I attended a program featuring Dr. Dennis Kimbro, author of *Think and Grow Rich A Black Choice*, and *Daily Motivations for African American Success: Including Inspirations from Famous African American Achievers*, who was also an entrepreneurship professor. The insight he shared about entrepreneurship resonated with me and ignited a "can do" fire within my heart. He was one of the most inspirational orators I'd ever heard. Before the event was over, I decided to pursue an MBA.

That journey took me halfway across the country. It led me to my friend and associate, Yolanda Spearman, a colleague in my business program who shared my entrepreneurial spirit. We compared our dreams while she created beautiful, one-of-a-kind jewelry designs. I was so inspired by her that I ended up working as her sales associate for a while. While she was designing and selling her line of jewelry, it sparked my desire to design and sell my own line of clothes. At 6'2", I had learned to be my own personal fashion designer. My mother taught me to design and sew. Her mother taught her, whose mother taught her. The list goes back more than a century to a garment industry on another continent. I even designed and sewed clothes for a small clientele of friends and family and wanted to expand my creativity into a business venture. I had a dream, just like Yolanda, to design and sell my own line. Designing was the easy part. It was the fun part. It was the thing that lit a fire in my belly. I loved it so much that I wanted to make a living at it, and I was willing to work hard...to apply the skills I learned in business school and work relentlessly to get it done.

I had a successful apparel line for over a decade before pursuing other dreams and goals. Through it all, Yolanda was motivating me with brilliant enthusiasm and encouraging me to unleash Relentless Execution. It is the principle that I apply to every other venture in my life.

Some of the things I love most about Yolanda are her passion for life, her work ethic, and her ability to motivate others. Yolanda rests in creativity. She delves into her passions during her downtime, where she becomes energized by expanding her dreams and possibilities. In addition to being a brilliant executive and entrepreneur, she's a coach. She gives you a playbook, helps highlight your talents, and encourages you to go for it. As an athlete, I can tell you; she's one of the best coaches I've ever had. When I think of her, I think of the ever-expanding universe where brilliance and light work together for the good of all things—both beautifully and **relentlessly**.

Her book, *Relentless Execution*, continues to motivate me, and I know it will inspire you as well. She uses personal stories about regular, everyday people who pursue their passions until they reach success at whatever they love and want to do. The key to that success is Relentless Execution. In addition to sharing stories, she provides a blueprint to help you get started, get unstuck, or just plain *motivate* you to achieve your dreams and goals. There is something extraordinary about Yolanda's ability to inspire those around her. Get ready, readers; you're about to go for a ride, and it's going to be a good one.

"*Do the best
you can until
you know better.
Then when you
know better,
do better.*"

MAYA ANGELOU

" I took the road less traveled and it made all the difference." Robert Frost

Introduction

T he energy we need to make our dreams come true comes from a well deep within. Passion drives our inner-power. Sometimes we don't understand what we are pursuing until we take a step back and actually look at what we call our dreams. That type of reflection is an integral part of our journey.

My daughter tripped up the basement stairs calling out, "Mommy, mommy! I found a book you wrote." She'd discovered an old journal lost and forgotten but full of memories and introspective thoughts from my much younger self.

I plopped down in the middle of the staircase and began to read. As I fingered through the bent pages, I struggled to read the loopy cursive letters scrawled across the pages. Tears filled my eyes. At that moment, I found myself again. I found my dreams scrawled out on these tattered pages in a blue jean journal.

I realized I hadn't changed all that much since my cursive writing days. In my first reflective moments with that journal, I held a gavel and a pointed finger. I pointed out each thing that I did not achieve. My heart dropped, and tears formed and rolled down my cheeks.

"Mommy, why are you crying? Is everything OK? What's on those pages that make you so upset?!" my daughter lamented. She held onto my neck, attempting to soothe me as I wept.

I brushed the tears off my face, hugged my little girl, and said, "I just found a magic book."

She wasn't going for it. As an 8-year-old, she knew something was off.

"No, Momma. Something happened in that book. Please tell me!" she pleaded.

I told her it was a book of my dreams, and somewhere along the way, I'd forgotten about some of them. At that moment, I put the gavel down in my mind and stopped pointing the finger at myself. I decided that it's OK to give my dreams some wiggle room—some space to grow and shift with the changes that come naturally in life. The spirit of my dreams and the essence of who I was way back when I wrote those dreams was still intact the day my daughter discovered that worn journal.

And who I am today remains the same as I work to execute those dreams.

The internal question I would pose to you is, have your dreams changed over the years? While I ask you this question, I feel forced to examine myself as well. I have started many businesses, but I've learned to ask myself, does the spirit of my dreams still live?

I began working on myself by looking at my past experiences. Here is my list of beginnings:

- Lon's Catalyst of Change—Business Consulting
- Yolanda's Greeting Cards
- Jewelry by YLON
- The Community Business Alliance
- Yomark Enterprises, Real Estate
- Yomark Performance Parts
- Ladies with Big Feet
- Yolanda's Voiceovers
- Knowtible—Training Company
- Easy Racing Solutions—Husband's Parts
- Why Voiceover Training
- Yolanda's Books

This list inspired me to reflect and ask myself *why I haven't been motivated enough to finish?*

As I pondered my goals, I started writing down the ones that I felt revolved around my real passions and purpose. Then one night at 3:00 a.m., my eyes popped open. I heard a voice in my head say, there is nothing wrong with your goals you need to *"execute"* better.

I faced myself in the mirror, this time without tears, realizing I lost my focus. I wanted something, and somehow I lost the definition of what that something was to me. Somewhere, I lost my "it"—the thing that gave me enough passion to follow through and finish it.

Welcome to my quest to figure out how to get my "it" back.

> *Note: As you read this book, you will notice that each chapter begins with a story or an interview with people just like you and me. The sections also end with a Relentless Execution Principle, which I refer to as REX Principles throughout the book.*

"Live a life without regrets."

UNKNOWN

CHAPTER 1

Do What Makes You Happy

This chapter makes me smile as I think back on it because I wrote it after standing in the doorway with a dinner plate in my hands—watching my husband, Mark, work on his favorite toy in the garage. He often tells me how he feels coming home from work, and I wanted a chance to share a glimpse into the mind of a husband who makes time to do what is expected of him—and what he loves.

MARK, HEAVY-REPAIR MECHANIC, DEPARTMENT OF TRANSPORTATION, THE HUSBAND IN THIS BOOK.

arrived home today, and my wife told me she needed me to build a rocket ship.

No, really, the dog jumped at the door as my hand touched the doorknob to enter the house. The kids were lined up with bikes to fix, toys to put back together, video games to join in, and so much more.

Honestly, I just got home from work, so none of this has happened yet. But I know it will happen as soon as I walk through that front door, which is why I am actually still sitting in my truck—wiping down my console and listening to the radio. I needed the beat of a good ole R&B song and some deep, relaxing breaths before jumping into my super-husband suit.

This is a story about me that I didn't even know was being written. My wife showed me this AFTER she wrote it. She told me it was *a book about regular people who do what they love.*

You see, I spend countless hours in the garage. My man cave looks good for a garage. I wish you could see it. I have a smart TV and stereo set up with surround sound. I cleared out the second stall to fit a nice table and chair set because sometimes I eat dinner out here when I am intensely working on a project. I even installed a furnace because Michigan winters are cold and I am tired of being out here with kerosene heaters in the winter.

The garage is my happy place. For fun, I drive a royal blue '79 Malibu with a pro-charged Chevrolet 400 cubic inch small block engine, that I built. I call her Mystique. I got that name from the character in the movie X-Men. I am an old- school drag racer, which means I can't tell you exactly how fast I go, but trust me, it's pretty darned fast. I have all the professional tools required to keep my car in tip top shape.

As I gaze at my racecar, I find myself remembering my last race. I recall each moment and each detail that I want to improve at the next event. I lose track of time as I formulate a plan of action. I have to be precise in racing. I write everything down so I remember exactly what I need to do to ensure that my car operates perfectly on the racetrack.

I always create a game plan first. You gotta be clear about the results you desire when you work on a big project like this or else you will be wasting time and money. And I have wasted a lot of both out here in this garage figuring that out. The process of doing my annual checks is long and tedious. These checks involve me checking spark plugs, replacing brake pads, reprogramming the electronics, and making sure everything is a perfect fit so that Mystique performs as expected. I examine every mechanical component of the car to repair, upgrade, or replace each piece, and yes, put them all back together again.

Working on my car makes me happy, or maybe I should say it makes my soul *content*. All I know is, I forget the time when I am here in my garage with my car. The only thing on my mind is one thought, when everything is back together, it will get a little better and go a little faster.

I smile to myself as I remember the last time I sat in the seat at the track, heart-pounding, 1,000+ horses behind me, the staging lane indicator lights in front of me, and the adrenaline inside me. In those seconds, I transform. My vision zeroes in on the light. Reaction time matters out here. I silence all other noises. It's me, the track, and the staging light. I hear my heartbeat as I wait for that titillating moment when the indicator displays green, and I greedily smash the gas pedal.

These races honestly only last a few seconds. And still, those seconds are worth the hundreds of hours I spend in that garage each year—building the best race car that I can—to get the PRECISE results that I want for those few moments of my life. I will indeed walk into my beautiful home in a moment and build my wife a rocket ship, fix every broken toy, and rub my little Yorkie's belly too. When I finish it all, I get to tinker on my royal blue '79 Malibu named "Mystique." It's my man-toy, and when I am out there working, it makes my heart happy.

DO WHAT MAKES YOU HAPPY

Find your flow.

This book is about regular people who have embraced Relentless Execution as a part of everyday life. As you read, I want you to understand that you are like each of these people, too. It's not about being rich or having a title that you can brag about—or creating a fancy new business. It is about finding your "happy place"—or the place where you enter the psychological state of flow where time doesn't matter so much. It's about delving relentlessly into the energy that drives your passion, which is more about the thrill of the thing than the thing itself. This is technically called "*psychological flow.*"

Mihaly Csikszentmihalyi, one of the original researchers of the psychology of flow, describes the state of flow like this

> "*The best moments in our lives are not the passive, relaxing times… The best moments usually occur if a person's body or mind is stretched to its limits in a voluntary effort to accomplish something difficult and worthwhile" (Csikszentmihalyi, 1990).*"

When I stood in the doorway, watching my husband lie on the cement floor of the garage, the temperature was 58 degrees. I nagged him a bit to come in before bringing out his dinner. He laughed and told me he was fine—just set the food on the small, black, bistro table sitting in the middle of the floor. He never looked at me. I stood there, wondering if I should push him to come into the house. As I observed him, I saw him humming and muttering to himself. Honestly, I could have thought he was "Cuckoo for cocoa puffs," but I smiled instead, realizing the first principle of this book.

Find a passion that makes you happy enough to fix your racecar while lying on a hard cold cement floor, in the middle of the winter, humming tunes just to be sure you get your car fixed right.

This brings us to the first principle:

REX PRINCIPLE #1:
DO WHAT MAKES <u>YOU</u> HAPPY

A poll conducted by Gallup, a global analytics company, of over 30,000 full and part-time U. S. employees discovered that only 34% of these workers were engaged on their jobs. This indicates that most people don't like what they do.

Life is too short to spend most of it doing something that you do not like. You owe it to yourself to do something that makes you happy. I am talking about so happy that you, like my husband, would give up hours upon hours working in the garage in the winter, spring, summer, and fall to experience complete satisfaction and fulfillment. Sometimes we feel like we don't deserve it, but we are wrong. We deserve to have joy and be fulfilled.

- Sift through the noise and uncover what makes you happy.

- Joy isn't thrust upon you. It evolves with you as you discover what you really like.

My husband decided being the best person for his family meant making time to do what he loves. He is not an entrepreneur. He enjoys his day job. He also values himself enough to find the time to pursue his passion.

What actions will you embrace to move your vision forward? This is all about you. Do what makes YOU happy.

As a reminder the first REX Principle we covered is:

REX Principle #1: Do What Makes YOU Happy

"Be like a postage stamp stick to one thing until you get there"

JOSH BILLINGS

CHAPTER 2

Find Your Focus

I sat in the kitchen, eating the last remnants of pound cake from Christmas dinner, the floors still littered with wrapping paper from yesterday. The smell of freshly brewed coffee was heavenly. I inhaled as I chewed the last bits of buttery crust from the pound cake and gazed out at the snow-covered porch through my window. The snow looked serene from my perch in the tall kitchen chair. I hugged my enormous mug of coffee, sighing with relief as the children slept soundlessly. The house felt warm and cozy. I whispered a prayer for my husband as he started up his truck to begin his trek to work in the middle of this fresh snow storm.

Eventually, I gave up my perch in front of the window and began picking up the mess from yesterday. As the day progressed, I relished the moments of putting batteries in new toys and watching the kids run through the house, playing in their pj's all day. I prepared a dinner of leftovers from our big Christmas spread the day before.

When the phone rang, I couldn't find it. No matter how long I live through Michigan winters, I still feel trepidation when my family is out on the roads in the snow. I ran frantically around the kitchen, searching for my cell phone. Finally, panting, I saw his number on the line, and I sighed with relief.

Mark's voice sounded different. I immediately asked if he was OK.

He paused and said, "Well, I need a new truck."

His response baffled me for a minute. Then I asked him, "What happened?"

He told me the story of his truck sliding on the icy roads and flying uncontrollably across the expressway, slamming into one wall, and rolling back onto the highway. The only thing that saved him from a major calamity was the time of the accident. Being the day after Christmas there weren't many cars on the road.

The problem was that he needed a new truck immediately. Over the next few days Mark and I searched for a new vehicle. It was now almost a week after Christmas, inventory was limited, and Mark could not find the truck he wanted in our budget.

I could only think of one person who could help us. He was the owner of one of the motorcycle dealerships that I knew pretty well. He also had strong ties with a Chrysler dealership. I called him to get some advice.

I recanted the story of what happened, and he said, "Can he drive the truck?"

I told him, "No, the truck is at the body shop, and they said it's totaled. He is in a rental car."

George said, "Give me five minutes, and I will call you right back."

Do you know how long five minutes is when you don't know what somebody is doing? I will tell you it felt like hours!! He called back as promised and said, "Okay, I need you to follow my instructions exactly." He proceeded to tell my husband which dealership to go to and who to ask for when he got there. The only issue was that my husband needed to get there before the store closed, and it was 25 miles away—in the snow. My husband had less than an hour to make it.

He did! He got to the dealership 20 minutes before they closed. They knew who he was when he got there. They rolled out the red carpet for him like he was famous. They hosted him like an old friend. He finished the paperwork after the dealership closed. They arranged to return the rental car for him and getting his trade from the body shop. He drove home in his new Ram truck, the precise one that he wanted. When my husband walked through the dealership's door, he said George had already called ahead to make sure the right people handled everything from start to finish. They gave him impeccable customer service.

I WANT YOU TO MEET GEORGE DE LA NUEZ, OWNER, WOLVERINE HARLEY-DAVIDSON, WHO SHARES HIS THOUGHTS ABOUT RELENTLESS EXECUTION.

I come to this dealership every day. I meet with customers and handle a host of other business tasks and challenges. Sometimes, I feel like a psychologist. Everyone takes a moment to sit down and share their thoughts with me. I know that this is where I am supposed to be. I get the rare opportunity to enhance others' lives, and for that, I am grateful. Truthfully, I start every day just like anyone else. I get out of bed, thank God for a new day, workout, and go to work.

My story is like so many others. I started as a salesperson in the automotive business. Then I moved up to become the sales manager. Eventually, somebody noticed my complete commitment to excellence. It didn't hurt that I was a dedicated salesman. I focused on my goals and serving my customers. I never missed a sales goal they threw at me. One man believed in me and gave me a shot in management. It was probably the best thing he ever did because our team outperformed everybody. We transformed that old car dealership into one of the top-performing dealerships in the country.

I worked long, hard hours—staying positive and focusing on my goals. I dreamed of owning my own dealership one day. Over time, while I worked all of those long hours I realized I made these owners a lot of money, and I needed to figure out how to transition from being an employee to an employer. The only problem was, I didn't have the capital required to purchase a dealership.

To understand why this is all significant, I want people to have a glimpse into my quest to ownership. In 1966, my family fled Cuba, escaping Communism with just the shirts on our backs. We arrived on what was called the "freedom" flights. I am still amazed that my father left everything he owned behind in Cuba to start over with absolutely nothing in America. I come from humble means, yet my parents instilled in me the crazy idea that I could do or become anything I wanted. They were resilient people who taught me 3 key principles that have guided me throughout my life. They taught me to:

1. Focus on my goals.

2. Work hard.

3. Do everything with Integrity and Appreciation.

As a result of these standards and the grace of God, I accomplished great things in life. Eventually, the owner of a large dealership on the other side of town noticed my achievements, reached out to me, and invited me to work for him at his car dealership. Five years later, an opportunity materialized, and I was blessed to be part of the inaugural leadership team at Wolverine Harley-Davidson. This dealership quickly evolved into the flagship motorcycle dealership in Michigan.

When I first started working there, I was the general manager. I hired whomever I could find that was willing to work hard and learn fast. I invested a lot into my people to build them up and help them grow into their potential. As a result, there were days I would pull up to the dealership, and we had people lined up outside, waiting for the doors to open.

Remember, I had a goal, to own a dealership. I proved myself year after year, achieving sales goals, creating excellent customer relationships, and winning Harley-Davidson awards, but I still didn't own the dealership.

Sometimes people need to understand that you have to be willing to do whatever it takes to make your personal dreams come true. My determination led me to leave Wolverine Harley-Davidson for a few years to lead another dealer group in Ann Arbor and Brighton, Michigan. After these years away, I met with the owner of Wolverine Harley-Davidson again. This time, I became a partner and the sole operator of Wolverine Harley-Davidson.

Yolanda, I want people to know that focus is one crucial key to success. You also need passion. I don't apologize for my enthusiasm because it keeps me going when times get tough. One more point that I feel needs to be said, you need to love what you do. **"If you don't love what you are doing, then quit now, and stop making other people miserable."** George De La Nuez

Never forget where you began.

When I started as the dealer/operator, I determined in my heart not to forget that people all begin at the same place. Customers and employees deserve to be treated with integrity and appreciation. It's good for business, and it's also good for humanity. Remember where you started, it will help you remain humble when you experience success.

Follow through.

I got to where I am today by being a student of the business. I created a plan. I worked hard, and **I followed through**. Sometimes, the most critical piece of the puzzle that many motorcycle dealers miss is that they just don't follow through—details matter. **Relentless Execution often seals the deal.**

I follow through every day, and I give thanks to God because nothing would be possible for me without His grace, and I know that I couldn't do this by myself. Success is a team sport. **I have the best managers on the planet.** They get me, and they make everything possible.

"People don't decide their future; they decide their habits, and their habits determine their future."

I have 62 people who replicate my sales processes. Whenever I introduce a new directive to my teams, I keep in mind these things:

1. Explain to your team why you are in business. People have a psychological need to understand why they are doing what they do. (*Read Start With Why by Simon Sinek*)

2. Give each team/person clearly defined goals.

   ✓ Create repeatable processes that can be tracked and measured.

   ✓ Set clear moral boundaries.

   ✓ Ensure your teams know **how** you expect them to treat customers and **how** you commit to handling them.

   ✓ Encourage a positive can-do attitude.

   ✓ Stay focused.

   ✓ Hold everyone accountable, even yourself.

My employees are driven. When I say that, I mean they are centered around one objective: their department's performance. Their goals are visible in every office, the supervisors and team members consistently visualize their expectations. I check in with the managers weekly on their performance to plan. On the off chance that they are not poised to make an objective, we talk about it as a group and work together to sort out how we can support a struggling department. We do this process religiously. These types of routines enable me to run one of the top performing dealerships in the country.

When Yolanda told me about this book, I said, that's a book about my life. To be successful in life, you must be relentless.

My name is George De La Nuez, and I am from Cuba. I am the owner/operator of Wolverine Harley-Davidson, the best Harley-Davidson dealership in the state of Michigan. Of course, I am biased, and unapologetically so.

One last point: You gotta put in the work.

Accomplishment happens when you put in the work. In all actuality, finishing the work is the hardest part. Business is not easy, and success is not instantaneous. It takes versatility, resolve, determination, faith, and patience.

Some people fixate on money, and I admit it is an essential factor—but it's not all about money. If you do it just for the money, you will give up long before you reach success, and you may miss some critical moments that can enrich your business and life. Find your focus. Put in the work, and you will experience success.

George's words of wisdom lead us to our next principle of Relentless Execution.

REX PRINCIPLE #2:
FIND YOUR FOCUS

As mentioned in the foreword and introduction, I am one of those people who is considered a serial entrepreneur. For those of you who don't know what this means, serial entrepreneurs love to start businesses. We are visionaries and founders. As I shared, I have owned many businesses. One of the most important lessons I learned through those business experiences was that I had too many.

It's not wrong to dream. Dreams provide us with a sense of purpose and help us imagine our creative potential. We should be imaginative and within our musings we need to search for that enlightened idea. Narrow down your big list of ideas to the one you want to focus on today. In the book, **The One Thing**, it talks about the extraordinary results you can achieve when you can quiet your mind and direct your energy to one goal or passion you want to achieve.

There is a commercial by Michael Jordan called "Maybe It's My Fault" that embodies this particular point. We all know Michael Jordan as one of the greatest basketball players of all time, but he didn't get to be the best by being flighty. He buckled down, zeroed in on one goal, and evolved into a living legend. Although he reveled in other interests such as golf and baseball, he focused on basketball. Sure, he had other ventures in his life, but he started with a singular focus to perfect one thing. He worked on it daily with Relentless Execution.

I know some of you out there understand my dilemma. I enjoy imagining what could be because it pushes me and gives me energy. Over the years, I have learned that ideas are remarkable indicators of our ability to see the future.

The execution of the ideas we spend time pontificating about separates the good from the great and the dreamers from the achievers. Zero-in on the one objective you **need** to accomplish and give it the focus it deserves. *So, what's it going to be? What is that one thing you need to complete?*

As a reminder the REX Principles we have covered are:

REX Principle #1: Do What Makes YOU Happy

REX Principle #2: Find YOUR Focus

"Courage is not having the strength to go on. It's going on when you don't have the strength."

THEODORE ROOSEVELT

CHAPTER 3

Sometimes You Have to Pick Up Poop

The sweat rolled down my neck like I had just jumped out of a swimming pool. I panted for breath, looking for my water bottle for a moment of respite. Brandishing my garden shovel to my husband to get his attention, I yelled for him to bring me a cold bottle of water from the freezer.

I prepared for this. I loved it. I play in the dirt. I create gardens of roses, stone croppers, daylilies, maiden grasses, and daisies. I started with a shovel and a vision, and an overgrown clay rocky area. I decided to revive my struggling landscape.

While I worked, a lady wearing a huge smile waved to me and walked over. We were new to the neighborhood, and she wanted to introduce herself to me. She told me her name was Amy and asked me what I was planting. We chatted. I sweated. Then she said, "After all of this hard work, you and your husband should come on over for a beer to cool off. We live right behind you, just past the big bushes."

Mark (the husband) and I went. We are always cautious about new people, but Amy went out of her way to make us feel welcome.

She introduced us to her family, and they all received us with open arms. As a Black family in a suburban neighborhood, you never know how people feel about newcomers. Amy and her family treated us like regular people. We have many neighbors who ended up being as kind as Amy. Yet, Amy went out of her way to include us in the little neighborhood circle, and her small acts of kindness made a big difference.

THIS STORY IS ABOUT AMY VANDECAR, VICE PRESIDENT, HENRY FORD HEALTH SYSTEM, AS SHE REFLECTS ON HER ROAD TO SUCCESS.

I walked carefully across the manicured lawn, smiling as I passed my new flower bed filled with hydrangeas. As usual, I was dodging vast piles of poop from my two beautiful golden retrievers, Ginger and Maggie.

They bring me so much joy—and they leave me just as much poop to pick up behind them. My dogs represent all that is good to me, and their innocence lifts my spirits, even when I have to pick up their poop.

While I walked, I thought about my workday. Sometimes I feel like I work too much. I go to bed at night, contemplating work, and I wake up thinking about things at work. I finally got the position that I wanted and I hope that with the new responsibilities I am able to implement some of the positive changes that I have been trying to move forward. I want to make a difference in life and at work and I hope this is the start of a new beginning.

Yolanda has been waiting to find out what occurred after my numerous interviews for the role and I should let her know the good news. I truly earned this promotion.

After our gleeful hugs of celebration Yolanda asked me to tell her how I climbed the corporate ladder. Her question made me laugh a little because my answer is really pretty boring. I don't have an extravagant example of overcoming adversity. I buckled down, worked hard, and got the job. I believe people advance when they focus on their goals and pursue them relentlessly. When you asked me what I would say to people who want to experience success in Corporate America. I would say become a relentless problem solver, be resilient and flexible and a little lucky and hopefully your work will speak for you.

I also feel compelled to point out that most high achievers can't do great projects alone. We depend on a profoundly equipped group of individuals. I think it's ideal to surround yourself with people who have the same can-do spirit that you have and you need a good boss. You need a boss who understands your potential and wants to see you grow.

I talk a lot about hard work because I am a simple person. I want people to understand that hard work with clear intent is how you climb the corporate ladder. If you are not busy achieving a goal or completing a job, you are wasting time. Don't waste your time doing things that don't matter. All of your actions should push you toward the achievement of your goals.

No free lunch.

I also want people to know that there is no free lunch out there. Managers notice hard workers. Good leaders recognize talent.

Understand your skills and find opportunities to put them on display.

Get over it.

If I had a chance to give my younger self advice on advancing in Corporate America, I would say, stay focused and remember that we all experience crappy situations at work. Pick up the poop and get over it. Don't hold on to things that can derail you from your objective; press on, despite the challenges you will face. And trust me, you will face challenges. My final point is as primary as they come. Do "the work." Most people fail at "the *doing*" part of work. Don't let that be you.

Amy's reflections lead us to our third principle of Relentless Execution.

REX PRINCIPLE #3:
SOMETIMES YOU JUST HAVE TO PICK UP POOP

Let's just call a spade a spade. Some work is just crappy. I hate billing and collecting money from people. I do voiceovers for several companies, and the most challenging part about each job for me is following up and sending customers the bill. When it comes to anything I create, I feel timid about accepting praise and asking for money. Back in college, when I sold jewelry, I called my friend Marlena to help me because I sucked at selling my stuff. Customers bombarded me, and I was not too fond of that part of the business. My friend, Marlena, jumped in and did the hard parts for me. If you met Marlena, you would understand why that is an oxymoron. I am gregarious and she is more soft spoken by nature. Today, when I do voiceovers, there is no one to jump in and sell for me.

Guess what? I learned that the hard parts never go away, and sometimes you just have to do the stuff you hate.

When you hear a success story, remember you do not hear the part about all the poop they had to pick up along the road to success. Pick up the poop, wash your hands, and keep it moving. It's just part of the process on your road to success.

What poop do you need to pick up to get to your dream? If you are like me, you may not like doing the paperwork to get your business started, yet it's a necessary part of the process. You may have to pay more taxes when you get that big promotion that you worked so hard to get. Yes, this is all part of the journey to success. Sometimes you do have to pick up poop. Are you willing to get your hands dirty?

As a reminder the REX Principles we have covered are:

REX Principle #1: Do What Makes YOU Happy

REX Principle #2: Find YOUR Focus

REX Principle #3: Sometimes You Have to Pick Up Poop

"To begin with the end in mind means to start with a clear understanding of your destination. Know where you're going so that the steps you take are always in the right direction."

STEPHEN COVEY

CHAPTER 4

Begin with the End in Mind

The rain pummeled the windshield on our Ford Explorer as we crept down the residential street, searching for the right address. My pregnant belly touched the dashboard as my husband graciously handled the many Michigan potholes that plagued our streets after every winter. Finally, we pulled into the crumbling driveway of a simple traditional colonial. The grass was overgrown and browning. The flowerbeds were full of rocks. The puddle in the backyard had ducks sitting in it like it was a pond.

When my husband looked over at me, I shook my head vigorously, "no," and told him to jump out and take a quick look at the house, and we could keep going. I was not about to waddle my hugely pregnant self into a place that didn't offer much curb appeal. Our house hunting adventure could keep on moving past this one.

My husband stayed focused and encouraged me to get out and take a quick look. Since we drove through the rain to find the house, it would be a waste if we didn't give it a chance and at least take a quick look. Besides, if he went in alone and liked it, he would have to come back and get me anyway. So, I got out and shuffled down the narrow sidewalk, rolling my eyes as the rain soaked me.

When we opened the door, our mouths dropped open. We stood in the foyer mesmerized at the hominess of this quaint home. The all-natural hardwood floors sparkled, the picture windows allowed a ton of natural light to fill the living room, and the newly added speckled granite countertops cinched the deal -- we knew this was our dream home.

When the sellers accepted our offer, I cried like a baby. Then I walked back into our lovely empty home that I just bought and realized I wanted all new furniture. Armed with my newborn daughter Zoe, who had joined us in person only three months ago, I grabbed my mother, loaded up the baby, and went shopping.

IN THIS STORY, MEET DELORES, MY MOTHER, RETIRED DETROIT PUBLIC SCHOOL LIBRARIAN, AND THE LADY WHO GAVE ME MY DARING "LET'S TRY THIS" ATTITUDE.

When we got to the furniture store, I strolled in with a list, a budget, and the determination of a hungry dog to get what I wanted. We decided to sneak in through the back door to avoid the inevitable furniture salesperson. Right after the door clanged shut behind us, my mom quipped, "Oh Lord, here they come." We tried to hide behind tall dressers to keep from being spotted, but it didn't work. At that point, we attempted to plan B by hastening our retreat, as we felt like food for a school of hungry piranhas. Honestly, I think furniture shopping is worse than car shopping. Once you step foot in that furniture showroom, you are fresh meat, and the salespeople pounce on you from all sides, barely giving you a chance to raise your hands in surrender.

The crafty salesman sitting near the door at the back of the store jumped up from a chair like, "I gotcha!" and said, "Hi, what can I help you find today?"

If you are like my mother and me, we tried to keep each other engaged in conversation hoping he would go away, he just patiently waited.

Finally, my mother turned and said firmly, "Just looking!"

The salesperson undauntedly persisted. "OK, well, at least tell me what you are looking for so I can point you in the right direction."

We gave in, since it was a fair question, and said, "We are looking for a couch."

"OK, couches are to the left, just past those dining room sets," he responded. "I will be just over here if you need me." We quickly nodded and began almost jogging to the area he pointed out, avoiding eye contact at all costs.

Notice how the salesperson gently leads us through the sales process.

People in sales focus on what they want, and they follow a process to get to a specific outcome. They begin with the end in mind. The first milestone is to get the customer to talk. The second goal is to gain trust. ("I won't bother you; I will be here if you need me.") When the salesman says he won't bother you and follows through by not bugging you, this is part of a well-thought-out strategy to quickly build trust with customers. The salesperson then may loiter (often hidden behind some corner) near you, as opposed to directly engaging you, so that you can see them actively "not bothering you" but available to answer any pressing questions from you.

Then that mysterious salesperson we met at the door somehow showed up in our path, right as we were getting up from a couch that caught our eye. He glided over to my mother and I and said, "Did you know that this couch also has a massage feature? I see you are a new mom. I am sure you would enjoy this feature. Just press the red arrow twice and tell me what you think."

Here is the next step in the sales process. The salesperson introduces a feature that we might like, and then he shows us how to use it.

Notice how smoothly we are moving through the process. Next, I asked the salesperson a question. "Is this a durable couch? As you can see, I have a new baby, and I want to make sure it's safe as well."

The salesperson, at this point, brings out a pad of paper and starts making notes. They have successfully ushered you into the discovery portion of the sales process.

The salesperson then says, "Would you like me to get this written up for you? We only have three left, and this one is the last one in the color gray." Ding, ding, ding! He introduced scarcity into the sales process to get me to feel the need to buy today. This was a trial close.

Finally, he offered me some information that I didn't know. The salesperson said something like, "How were you planning to pay for this purchase? And the reason I ask is because we are offering 60 percent off on certain items. This couch happens to be one of those items, which is why we only have three remaining in stock." I thought back to my list and my big, beautiful, new, empty house. I liked the couch and didn't want to miss out on the sale, and my mom was still enjoying the massage feature.

Therefore, I went ahead and bought the entire living room set because it was "less expensive" to buy it this way, and I had a list and a big, new, empty house to fill. The salesperson already knew that we would say, "Just looking," when he first met us. He'd probably heard it hundreds of times every day, but he did not allow our initial rejection to derail his process.

The critical point to learn from this is don't walk away at the first sign of trouble.

Our personal quests can benefit from the principles this salesperson applied. We all face obstacles with the understanding that if we follow through with our process, we will experience success. Be like this salesman who didn't take our initial brush-off as defeat. He didn't walk away at the first sign of trouble. He committed himself to the process, even though it was uncomfortable. If he had left us at "just looking," we may have purchased less, we may not have purchased at all, and most certainly, he probably would not have earned the commission for our sale.

He understood all of this before my mother and I entered the building. He began with the end in mind. The moment that the salesman said hello to us at the furniture store's back door, he saw us as buyers and imagined himself selling us something today. He put us through the sales process before our first hello.

This leads us to the fourth principle of Relentless Execution.

REX PRINCIPLE #4:
BEGIN WITH THE END IN MIND

Just like the salesman in my story, you must begin with the end in mind. See yourself fulfilling your dream or passion. Imagine yourself sitting at the table with your team, even though you may not have one yet. Imagine yourself running past the finish line of your first marathon, even though you can barely walk to the corner right now. Think about your dream. When you see your plan, are you envisioning the process to help make that dream come true? Can you visualize the finished product? Are you beginning with the end in mind? (Sometimes, knowing what the finished product looks like keeps you going when things get tough.)

Have you written down your ideas? Any thoughts or musings that live only in your head reside in a place called your imagination. Hope is not a plan. Making your vision become a reality requires a detailed blueprint. Visualize the result and work backward to get started. For example, you want to open an online store and become an Amazon Reseller making a million dollars a year. Here is how a simple plan may look:

- ✓ Step One: Create a business – Give your business a name and structure.

- ✓ Step Two: Create an Amazon Seller Account.

- ✓ Step Three: Research the category you think you may want to choose as your Niche and select your niche.

- ✓ Step Four: Research specific products you want to sell and find product sourcing.

- ✓ Step Five: Determine how much money you need to develop your brand and launch your product.

✓ Step Six: Develop a pricing strategy and create your product listings.

✓ Step Seven: Marketing Your Product.

Now it's your turn to write down a small sketch of your plan. We dive more into this in the workbook, but why wait. Get started now. What did you write down? Remember, a plan can begin with a word, a phrase, a list, or a note—which will eventually evolve into a more formal written outline.

I thought about writing a book when a particular phrase popped into my mind, and I wrote it down. The term was "Relentless Execution." Actually, I was on an airplane half-asleep, and this book popped out, almost literally. I have to tell you this story. I was on a plane heading to a work meeting. We had all gotten comfortable in the sky and the attendants were beginning food service. The flight attendant handed me a cup of seltzer water with lime, and I asked for an extra napkin. I sipped my drink and gazed out at the clouds. I was on my way to another sales training class. I thought to myself *if only I could get my dealers to follow through with their ideas.* Then I started thinking about myself and how hard the execution of plans can be and then the idea hit me, I thought to myself; *maybe I should write this down,*" so I struggled to find an ink pen in the black hole of a purse I carried with me. Once I found the ink pen, words spilled onto that tiny napkin. I was sitting in the window seat, and the words just kept coming. I filled up the napkin and needed more paper. Stuck by the window, I gingerly tapped my dozing seatmate and said I needed to get up to use the restroom. I went to the back of the plane and beckoned a flight attendant and said, "I am an author, and I feel inspired right now. Do you have any paper?"

"Oh, how cool," she responded. "I want to be a writer someday," and blah blah.

I interrupted her and said, "How about a pile of napkins?"

She handed them to me, and I almost ran back to my seat. I know that man sitting next to me thought I was crazy as I filled 17 napkins with chapters 1, 2, and 3 of this book. Yup, all of this came from a cup of seltzer water and lime. Imagine what I would have burped up if it had been something more potent.

Start by creating a list and then outlining what you think you'll need to do to get your idea off the ground, out of your mind, and into action. Don't think about the money yet. If you feel inspired and want to go for it right now, get started; more power to you. The chapter is ending anyway. And I have a pet-peeve about the best things being at the back of the book. Go ahead and get started now!

I heard this quote from a basketball coach, Tony Blackwell, which resonated with me. He said, "Expectation without Explanation leads to Exasperation." People love telling you to plan, but they rarely tell you what should be in the plan and how to execute these ideas. I am giving you thought starters, but the work is still going to be the hardest part.

The reason I say write them down is to make your goal more tangible. Here are some examples of how writing out your thoughts can make them more real.

- Author Books. (Write the titles of the potential books.)

- Invest in Real Estate (Where do you want to invest?

What types of property do you want to own? Vacation, flip, rental, and why?)

- Own a Boutique or Store (Write the name of the store.)

- Create a Product (What is it? Who needs it? What problem does it solve? Who else is making it? Why is yours better, cheaper, or easier to use?)

When you write these items down, the next action is to start thinking about **how** you can begin developing your dream. Start by asking yourself a few poignant questions like:

1. Is this dream doable for me right now? Yes/No/Maybe

2. Do I want to commit to owning and operating a business or do I like the idea of having a business?

3. What can I do today to test my idea without wasting a lot of money?

Once you seriously weigh your options, then you take a leap of faith from the idea phase into the development phase and then finally into the execution phase.

Move forward purposefully.

- Think about the simple things you can do every day to move one step closer to your goal? If you want to get an activity done, you need to give it priority on your to-do list.

- Will you work on your personal goals every day, every week, or every month? *Do not condemn yourself if you don't work on your dreams every day. You don't need to water a flower every day for it to bloom. Set a target for yourself and work on it at your pace -- Period. Don't let the dream die in your head.*

I gave you a couple of thought starters, and now I want to share some concrete tasks that you can start doing now to keep progressing toward your goal.

- ✓ **Start small by Researching your Industry.**

- ✓ **Get your business name registered officially.**

- ✓ **Determine the structure of your business.**

- ✓ **Begin at the beginning.** If you want to sell cakes, start baking and selling cakes from your home.

- ✓ **Research** the laws and permits you need for your business to be in legal compliance. Avoid unnecessary fines and complications. You can often find a lot of this information on your state's website.

- ✓ **Share your idea safely.** Find a group of close friends you trust and who support your vision, or join a group of like-minded people. Talk with them, get their feedback.

- ✓ **Listen.** Sometimes your great idea sucks. A true friend will let you down gently. You want open and honest feedback.

- ✓ **Be open.** If your friends love you, they will tell you the truth, even if you don't want to hear it. Accept constructive criticism and new ideas.

✓ **Write down what you think.** Be positive and realistic. If your business needs millions of dollars on day one, and you only have $10.00 in your savings account, maybe you can become a blogger/vlogger about the business. At the same time, you figure out how to raise capital, or perhaps you can consider partnering with someone.

✓ **Explore your options**. What are some other opportunities that you haven't considered?

If you want to own a franchise, start doing your research, find out how much capital you need. Consider getting a part-time job working for the franchise you may want to buy. I thought I wanted to make cookies for a living until I got a part-time job working at Mrs. Fields Cookies. Research is key.

Here are the words that no one ever wants to say out loud. It's OK if you decide that you never want to run a business. You may prefer to be the best employee at your job every single day. You may not be entrepreneurial, and if you are not entrepreneurial, then what is your passion project or hobby that brings you joy?

Did you always dream of learning to play the piano, or did you dream of owning a vacation home or having your artwork displayed at a gallery? Figure out what inspires you and begin with the end in mind.

As a reminder the REX Principles we have covered are:

REX Principle #1: Do What Makes YOU Happy

REX Principle #2: Find YOUR Focus

REX Principle #3: Sometimes You Have to Pick Up Poop

REX Principle #4: Begin with the End in Mind

"Success occurs when your dreams get bigger than your excuses."

ZIG ZIGLAR

CHAPTER 5

Your Inspiration Must Be Bigger than You

After about six months of marriage, at age 35, I woke my husband up in the middle of the night, declaring that I had a special dream. I shook him awake, eagerly exclaiming, "Mark, I had a dream that we are going to have a baby girl named Zoe. I feel like this is a dream from God preparing us for our future." My husband rolled over, looked at me like I was crazy, and went right back to sleep.

I never imagined the impact that this vision would have on my life. This dream became a nightmare before it became a blessing. I thought pregnancy would come naturally. People all around me popped up pregnant every day. My nieces and nephews shot out one after another at what seemed like an alarming rate, and yet I was childless.

61

THIS IS ME, UNEDITED, YOLANDA SPEARMAN, AUTHOR, TEACHER, SPEAKER, CORPORATE PROFESSIONAL, RELENTLESS DREAMER, AND PURSUER OF MORE.

When I reached 38 and still didn't have any children, I felt sorely disappointed. I believed with all of my heart that the dream I had was from God, and I could not understand why I didn't get pregnant. I drowned my sorrows in solitude and lifted my spirits by being the favorite aunt. It became a tradition to take my nieces and nephew to see every kids' movie as soon as it came out. We enjoyed many fun playdates, and I pretended that they were my kids.

The Bible says in Proverbs 13:12 that "hope deferred makes the heart sick," and oh, was my heart sick. I went to see an infertility doctor, and the journey of 1,820 days began. I experienced every treatment known at the time, including Clomid, insemination, IVF, IVF with ICSI, frozen embryo transfers, fertility acupuncture, fertility massages, and other holistic treatments. I did it all again and again and again until "no" became an echo that haunted my dreams. I heard "no" so often that I was certain I missed the message of that dream I had long ago, the one about my daughter Zoe.

After five years of trying, my husband tired of going into the fertility office to make sperm deposits, and he felt annoyed at me for being sad all the time. Then one day, I decided to stop trying to get pregnant. I finally gave in to the fact that maybe I would have to be a mother some other way. I cried a lot. The nurses, who were now like family, cried when I told them my decision, and they convinced me to try one last time before throwing in the towel.

We all (the nurses and I) begged the doctor to break her standard, conservative IVF protocol. We begged her to insert four eggs instead of the medically recommended three, advising the doctor that this would be my very last attempt. The nurses coaxed her with me, and she got a little annoyed at us, but ultimately she relented. I got pregnant with three of the four eggs. Two of the embryos didn't survive, but one did. I kept the faith, and my doctor stayed in the fight with me. Her name is Dr. Jennifer Kaplan. I love that lady.

Did I mention that I was almost 40 years old, which is a geriatric pregnancy in baby birthing terms? Imagine my elation at the notice that I was pregnant.

I told Dr. Kaplan all about my dream of having a baby girl named Zoe. She doted on me. I think she felt sorry for me, but she played along with a game face. Since the pregnancy's announcement, I told Dr. Kaplan, I didn't want to know the baby's gender before it was born. I held onto the inspiration for my vision from five years before.

Then the worst happened. The Doctors did not think I would be able to carry the baby to full term. Since I was an older patient, the chances of all types of horrible things happening to my baby were excessively high. Because of the risks, I was hospitalized and put on bed rest for 3.5 months. I had to lie flat on my back in the hospital. All my hopes wavered, and it was my family that helped me keep the faith. I believed that I was having a girl named Zoe because I saw her in a dream. I felt this was divine providence. And at the same time, the doctors prepared me for the worst.

I held on to the vision that I would have a little girl. All of this happened before "gender reveals" were popular. I found out the gender a few weeks before the baby was born. At week 38, Zoe Spearman was born— the little, 4.6-ounce miracle. Before her birth, I wondered about the significance of the name Zoe (pronounced Zoey). I researched it a bit while lying in my hospital bed and discovered that in Greek, her name means "the life of God."

Would you believe that I did this entire process one more time? I decided that I didn't want Zoe to be alone? There were no visions involved this time around. I wanted my daughter to have a sibling. My poor husband objected feverishly and would only allow me to try with one egg. I have to tell you; I almost divorced his butt over this. It took four eggs to get one baby, and now he wanted me to try with just one egg. I was pissed, but I did it. And it worked. I got a beautiful, healthy baby boy named Marcus Spearman. He is just as much of a miracle as Zoe because I was in the hospital on bed rest while pregnant with him for 21 weeks, and every doctor expected him to be a preemie. He made it to 38 weeks and was born healthy and strong with no issues.

Here is my next point. Our dreams don't always manifest the way we think.

I share this story because we all have aspirations, and they don't always happen the way we think they will, but we can and should remain inspired.

Next, give your vision an identity.

Your inspiration needs to drive your actions. For me, it was my dream about Zoe. I believed that it was a message from God. I felt so strongly about the vision that no one could sway me. I remember calling all the embryos "Zoe" before the doctor implanted them. I named them to give them an identity and to imagine a life.

I said this before, and it bears stating again, find a community of supportive people who will believe in you.

Some may ask if I had doubts, and the answer is YES. I remember calling one of my sister-friends—crying uncontrollably, filled with doubt. My friend told me to hold onto my faith. My sister bought me a tiny green four-leaf clover onesie and hung it up on my hospital room's bathroom door as a faith extender. It always reminded me to keep my faith. The inspiration in my soul pushed me forward. When I could not find my voice, I found a community of friends and family who believed in me. They did not let me forget the dream.

This story leads us to our next principle of Relentless Execution.

REX PRINCIPLE #5:
YOUR INSPIRATION NEEDS TO BE BIGGER THAN YOU

Most businesses start because of a single passion. Henry Ford began his journey with inspiration. Early in his life, he started out tinkering with machines. Ford eventually got a job as a machinist working part-time for Westinghouse Engines. Then he moved to the Edison Illumination Company, where he quickly moved through the company's ranks. The Edison Company promoted Ford to lead engineer, which required him to be on call for 24 hours a day. Can you imagine working on your dreams while you are on-call 24 hours for your day job? He snatched any free time he could find to tweak his passion projects. In 1896, he finished his first invention called the quadricycle. It had a light metal frame with four bicycle wheels and a two-cylinder, four horsepower gasoline engine. Henry Ford did one thing differently than the other car manufacturers at the time. He sold his quadricycle *to make money* so that he could perfect his project and build more. This one practice would turn out to be what set him apart from other automakers.

Henry Ford believed an engine could be developed to carry people in a buggy, much like the train transported people across the country. Ford started his car business with a one-cylinder engine and was bankrupt in 18 months. After one more failed attempt, Henry and 12 investors finally created the company we now know as The Ford Motor Company. Mr. Ford failed forward for seven years until he finally found the winning combination for his vision.

Henry Ford lived a colorful life, much like the ones described in this book. He picked up a lot of poop and began with the end in mind. His inspiration pushed him forward, and he became known in history as a linchpin in the Industrial Revolution (*Corporate.Ford.Com*).

Take a second and think back on something that inspired you, and you tried it and failed? Did you sincerely love what you were doing? Did you give your idea 100 percent? Maybe you haven't tried anything yet. I was chatting with a person some time ago who told me that he did not have passion projects in his life. The thought of not having a passion for anything made me feel a little sad for him. Everyone needs something in their life that inspires them. Start a list and write down thoughts that permeate your mind. Maybe you will birth a movement? *Think about what fuels your passion. When is the last time you felt solely focused on a project? What inspired you? Is this inspiration big enough to carry you through good and bad times? Are you willing to pursue your passion until you finish it?*

As a reminder the REX Principles we have covered are:

REX Principle #1: Do What Makes YOU Happy

REX Principle #2: Find YOUR Focus

REX Principle #3: Sometimes You Have to Pick Up Poop

REX Principle #4: Begin with the End in Mind

REX Principle #5: Your Inspiration Must Be Bigger than You

"Success seems to be connected to action. Successful people keep moving. They make mistakes but they don't quit."

CONRAD HILTON

CHAPTER 6

Never Give Up

He barely made it up the 100 or so steps to the front porch. When he got there, he sat down for a second to slowly inhale. He thought to himself, it was getting increasingly hard to do simple things. Getting up each day felt like work. He loved being with his family but he didn't have the foggiest idea how long he could continue living like this. The specialists said his heart was damaged beyond repair, and to survive, he would need a new one.

As he eased himself down the familiar porch steps, he pondered the words of the doctors to himself. The Doctors are saying I need a heart transplant. Do they understand what that means to me? If I agree to this operation, I could die. If I don't agree to the procedure, I will eventually die. I can keep living and let fate have its way, or I can take a leap of faith and try this medical procedure that will literally remove my damaged heart, throw it away, and give me a new one from some unfortunate soul whose loss of life could potentially save mine. The specialists say when they do the transplant, they stop the functioning of all major organs during the procedure once they finish the transplant, they start the organs back up again and HOPE my body responds favorably. How do I make the right decision? Stepping out on faith is scary. It's like walking off a cliff understanding that your feet may not land on solid ground. But God is faithful. I didn't give up on Him and He didn't give up on me.

Looking back on those moments when I was asked to make this life-changing decision, I can't believe it has been over 20 years since the heart transplant and I'm glad I took that step of faith. I know if I had not gotten the surgery, I wouldn't have been here to see my ten grandchildren. I made a personal decision to never give up. As that old song says, I have my good days and my bad days, and I still have hills to climb but I won't complain. I am still here today because I still have something to say. For all of your readers out there, I want them to know their life is important. They matter to God. Don't give up.

IN THIS CHAPTER, READ ABOUT THE QUEST OF ONE OF MY BIGGEST SUPPORTERS: MY DAD, RAYMOND, RETIRED NATIONAL SERVICE OFFICER (DAV)

I was thinking back on everything that transpired before I received the heart transplant. It takes time to get a new heart. You put your name on a list, and then wait for a match. It could take a month, or it could take years. While I waited for the new heart, I decided to try to make the best of a bad situation and take my wife on a short vacation to Niagara falls. We made it to the falls. They are a true natural wonder, and yet for me, the walk through the parking lot to see them was literally breathtaking. As we began touring the area with every step, I felt like I could not breathe, which happens when you have congestive heart failure. By the end of the trip, I embarrassingly ended up in a wheelchair.

I survived fighting a war in Vietnam. Now I could barely stand on my own two feet because my heart was failing me.

It is funny how things link together.

No matter how hard life gets, never give up. I am not saying it's going to be easy. I am saying it is worth the fight.

When I was in active combat in Vietnam as a Marine, the war was horrible. We were young men who felt indestructible, and we were in a land we did not know, fighting people we could not see.

One day while my platoon was out scouting, a bullet flew out of nowhere and slammed into my chest, causing a near-fatal wound. I don't remember much after I went down. I thank God every day for the man who carried me out and got me help. Without him, I would not be here today.

Because of the severity of my wounds, I was not allowed to go back to active duty. I ended up running a Barbershop on the Military base. It is funny how things all link together. I went to barber school long before the Marines drafted me. I enjoyed cutting hair. The fact that I could make money while doing something I liked made it even better. I never imagined that I would end up doing something I loved in the Marines. Cutting hair was my official job.

I experienced crazy twists and turns in my life before I ultimately landed a career with the Disabled American Veterans (DAV) as a National Service Officer. I went from cutting hair to helping people get the benefits they needed to thrive in the world outside of war. I often counseled people while I cut hair. When I worked for the Disabled American Veterans (DAV), my job was as a National Service Officer whose role is a counselor. It's uncanny to see how the dots all connect. I worked for the DAV until my heart condition made it too challenging to get to the office every day, and I am still cutting hair.

Exercise your faith.

I helped many people throughout my career. My most challenging moment came when I had to admit that I could not help myself. When the doctors told me I needed the heart transplant, they forced me to exercise my faith. I had to trust God and believe that the doctors knew what they were doing.

I received a heart transplant in 2001. By the grace of God, I am still here. People need to realize that life is not a game. It is crucial to focus on what matters most. Too often, people get caught up in stuff that doesn't last. Live a life that is worth fighting for, and never give up.

My name is Raymond Callaway, and I am a Marine, a Purple Heart recipient, a son, brother, husband, and father. I made a vow that I will never give up, and I hope everyone reading this book will take a fresh look at their own life and re-focus on what matters.

Raymond's story leads us to the next Relentless Execution principle.

REX PRINCIPLE #6:
NEVER GIVE UP

If we look back over our lives and think things over, I am confident that each one of us can say that we have a testimony. There are times in all of our lives when we have been forced to exercise our faith. Sometimes our quest can be a matter of life and death as it was with my father, and at other times, it is about the quality of our lives and our purpose.

There are things we have done that we never imagined we could do. Give yourself credit for your successes. I ran a marathon. All my toenails turned black and fell off after it was over. My legs cramped because I was not hydrated enough as I ran it. My parents rolled me out in a wheelchair when it was over, but I did it. There is no shame in my game because I finished all 26.2 miles. What goal have you given yourself that you completed?

Heck, I even had a baby. I lost hope for a while during my quest to get pregnant, yet here I stand with two children and a dog. What one thing have you done that you doubted would ever happen for you?

I wrote a book. I did a voiceover. I created a work of art. What passions have you pursued that may be small but matter to you?

My point here is to start looking back over your life and list your accomplishments. Look at everything you have done. When you look at that list, how do you feel? I was doing a training session once about this, and someone said to me, "I don't know what to write down." Think more simply. You accomplish great things, and you don't give yourself credit. It's time to look back over your life and find those moments when you exercised your faith and never gave up.

Write down your list of wins. How do you feel about yourself? What's the one thing all of your accomplishments have in common?

You didn't give up. YOU DID THE WORK, and that's what Relentless Execution is all about!

As a reminder the REX Principles we have covered are:

REX Principle #1: Do What Makes YOU Happy

REX Principle #2: Find YOUR Focus

REX Principle #3: Sometimes You Have to Pick Up Poop

REX Principle #4: Begin with the End in Mind

REX Principle #5: Your Inspiration Must Be Bigger than You

REX Principle #6: Never Give Up

"A goal is a dream with a deadline."

NAPOLEON HILL

CHAPTER 7

"If You Can Dream It, You Can Achieve It," And Please Write It Down

picked up the phone and dialed the number. It rang a few times. I hadn't called her in so long; I didn't know if she would still take my calls. She was once my mentor, but that was long ago. Now she is coined as one of the most powerful women in corporate America by *Forbes Magazine*.

Right, as I was about to hang up the phone, I heard the familiar call of my name. "Yolanda," answered Telisa on the other end of the line. We chatted for a few fleeting moments. The following paragraphs are a summary of our brief yet powerful conversation.

First, let me interject that in life we meet people that make an indelible impact. Telisa is this person for me. Whenever I speak with her, I feel grounded. Every conversation with Telisa inspires me to do more. At the time of this writing, she held the Chief Marketing Officer's title for American Family Insurance.

Summary of Our Conversation

Yolanda: Telisa, how do you feel being the CMO?

Telisa: I feel the same way I have always felt. I still dream, Yolanda.

Yolanda: You have finally gotten the job of your dreams, what more is there?

Telisa: What are you saying? I have taught you better than that! I don't know about you but my purpose is bigger than a title. We have more to do. I want to make an impact on the lives of these people at this company. I want to help someone and hopefully through my job and with my title I am able to help more people, Yolanda. What have you been reading? Don't forget that you are created with a purpose. When we walk the earth we are planting seeds that others may tend but you should be mindful of your actions because they all matter.

Yolanda: Ok, I agree. I didn't forget. I am making a difference everyday, I hope.

Telisa: Hope is not a plan.

Yolanda: Ugh – Laughing.

Telisa: What are you reading?

Yolanda: I am reading Outliers by Malcolm Gladwell.

Telisa: That's a good one. I am going to send you a reading list. I want you to read them all and take notes. Do you have a planner?

Yolanda: Yes! I use the Happiness Planner.

Telisa: So do I! LOVE IT! We always need to make sure we keep our dreams alive. Never lose sight of who you are and why God created you. Listen, God will make room for your talents and your dreams. I have to go but it was so good catching up. Stay positive. Go check out my DreamBank.

We chatted a bit more about the concept of her "DreamBank." It is a system designed to help others embrace the possibility of their dreams through insurance. This system, she feels, is one of her notable achievements. She shared with me that she told the team about her vision and her team made it a reality. The mission of the DreamBank is to inspire, protect, and restore dreams. The Dream-Bank is a community dedicated to the pursuit of goals. They share success stories and encourage others to embrace their inspirations, and yes, this is an INSURANCE company.

Plan your work and work your plan.

One of the most exciting parts of Telisa's story is how she monetized the concept of the DreamBank for her organization. It's a feel-good success story for everyone involved. A key point to take away from this is that her team took the idea and made it happen. They mapped out what success looks like, and then, they did it.

Telisa also pointed out, the key to making your dreams come true is to plan your work and work your plan. She said she surrounds herself with people who are change agents. She ended the conversation by saying, "I want people on my team who can embrace a vision and run with it—people who are dreamers. Her final comments on the phone call to me were, "Yolanda, be faithful to your dreams. write them all down and take lots of notes. You never know what will fuel your inspiration. Oh, and one more thing. Read."

She ended the call coaching me as if our last mentor-mentee conversation happened just a few days ago. She sent me a picture with the list of leadership books to read as promised. I smiled to myself when I tapped the red button to end the call.

After my conversation with Telisa, I started thinking about my life. I wondered why she focused on me taking notes. She always has a message within a message. Then I started mulling over incomplete plans and goals that I never achieved. I realized that many of us:

1. Talk about our dreams and goals.

2. Create vision boards.

3. Get busy in life and move away from our plans.

I don't know if we forget about our plans or if we feel we like we will never achieve them but the "taking notes" part of her conversation had me thinking back to my journals. I started the book talking about the discovery of an old journal. I look back on it today and I am there. I see my past vision of myself and what success looked like to me back then. I am not doing everything I desired. I am achieving more than I gave myself credit initially. Writing down the plan allowed me to look back and see what I accomplished and what I did not. It has also given me a chance to begin again.

Why you want to write down your goals

For those of you wondering why we are so fascinated with the concept of creating your goals and writing them down.

When you take the time to detail your plans view this activity as a map leading you to a very specific destination.

When you write down your goals, research from Psychology Professor Dr. Gail Matthews, has shown that you are 42% more likely to accomplish them.

Telisa's words of wisdom lead us to our next Relentless Execution principle.

REX PRINCIPLE #7:
IF YOU CAN DREAM IT, YOU CAN ACHIEVE
IT, AND PLEASE WRITE IT DOWN

Set yourself up for success. Start at the beginning. Write down your vision. Begin to build your dream on paper. Start with the end in mind.

Here is an example of what I wrote down to help myself get started on this book. I did not get into detail. I drafted the outline. Some people will tell you to write out every detail. I am a note taker, like Telisa. I designed the layout for the first three chapters on napkins on an airplane, and then I went back and did the outline. Here is what I jotted down:

Write a book.

- Title of the book
- What is the story?
- What is the point?
- How can people act on it?
- What problem does the book solve?

- What's your goal with the message?

- What inspired you to write about this subject?

It's much easier to write down your goals than to start doing them. In the questions above, notice how I asked different types of questions: Who inspires you and why? In your outline or plan, you want to be true to yourself. You must understand your personal "why." If you do not know why you decided to do this thing, the probability that the next great idea will derail your dream is very high. For example, during the writing of this book, the global pandemic COVID-19 is happening. Everyone wears a mask when they are in public. If I were focused on the marketplace only, I would shift gears, stop writing, and start making masks because they are challenging to get. You can make a ton of money, and they are relatively easy to make. It is easy to lose focus if you don't understand the inspiration for your specific dream. *What is your plan?*

> *Disclaimer: I want every reader to know that you do not need a big, grandiose dream. You can be like my husband, Mark, who has a simple hobby that puts him in a state of flow and allows him to be his best self in all other walks of life. His dream is to go a little faster in the quarter-mile.*

As a reminder the REX Principles we have covered are:

REX Principle #1: Do What Makes YOU Happy

REX Principle #2: Find YOUR Focus

REX Principle #3: Sometimes You Have to Pick Up Poop

REX Principle #4: Begin With the End in Mind

REX Principle #5: Your Inspiration Must Be Bigger than You

REX Principle #6: Never Give Up

REX Principle #7: If You Can Dream It, You Can Achieve It and Please Write It Down

"*Surround yourself with people who see your value and remind you of it.*"

UNKNOWN

CHAPTER 8

Fuel Your Passion with a Network Who Supports You

My husband sidled up next to me while I picked weeds in my garden. He has a habit of starting random conversations with me when my hands are deep in the dirt. He started the conversation like this "Hey Yolanda, do you know why I need a special fuel for my car?" Here comes the lesson that I didn't request.

"Did you know that the average car drives around 17-21 seconds in a quarter-mile? Some performance cars like Corvettes or Mustangs burn higher octane fuel, so they can get that punch when they mash the gas and take off like a bullet. The fuel octane that these vehicles use is normally 92 or 93, and they can go as fast as 12 seconds in a quarter-mile. I use 116 Octane Fuel. Do you understand why it's so important to have the correct fuel?" My proverbial answer is "no, and I don't care," but this is his passion, I go along and say why?" Here is what I learned.

My husband uses 116 octane fuel because the intense pressure in his racecar engine would burn up lower octane fuel before the engine could start. His racecar goes around 8.0 seconds on a quarter-mile track.

His comments got me thinking; when you need to perform at your best and under an immense amount of pressure, you need higher octane fuel to function. If you have lower octane fuel, you could fail or even explode.

Surround yourself with people who give you the fuel you need to move at the pace you are trying to go. We all need people around us who can energize our lives. We need people who see through the facade and into our souls. *These people need to perform well under pressure.* When you plug into your support network, they invigorate you and motivate you to keep going when others give up.

I recently read an article about friendships and how they may change over time. The article talked about categories of friends beyond your bar buddies. People who truly understand your intentions and value your vision.

I have a small crew. My friends and family allow me to dream, and I feel free to imagine great things when I am with them. They see my potential. They grow with me. When I'm with them, I am invigorated and renewed.

Who is in your crew? Who do you go to when you need that special higher octane fuel? My friends support most of my endeavors (with some candid feedback). Over the years, they have been around for many of the businesses that I've started. Vulnerability is the hardest part for me. Listening to candid feedback from people who are gracious enough to look at things from different angles challenges my thought processes. Who do you allow to give you advice? Understanding who you respect is an essential question because you could have a great network, but it will never help you improve if you are unwilling to listen.

Sometimes it is a little scary for all of us to let people in. It hurts to hear that your brilliant idea doesn't shine as brightly to a valued friend or confidant. When people genuinely love you, they want you to succeed. The constructive criticism they offer is the higher octane fuel you need to win.

Mark's thoughts lead us to our next Relentless Execution principle.

REX PRINCIPLE #8:
FUEL YOUR PASSION WITH
A NETWORK WHO SUPPORTS YOU.

You need a community. Friends and family will help you through the rough times, and there will be turbulent times. They will give you the push that you need to stay focused, and then they will be right there, holding your hand (perhaps metaphorically) to watch your dream become a reality.

My husband pushes me beyond what I believe is possible. He sincerely believes in me. When I read him this book, he immediately burst out with, "It's a bestseller!" I told him that's because I talked about him in the book, and he said, "No, I think it's good."

My parents undauntingly support me and allow me to brainstorm with them, sharing thoughts, and getting feedback. Their support of my many ventures never wavers.

You need people who support you like this in your life.

Then there are the ones you share your secrets with, like my locker partner from high school, Marlin. I tell her my wildest dreams. I don't talk to these people every day. I plug in when I need to, and they plug in when they need to.

You will also find that you can't tell everyone about your dreams. Some people are dream killers. They don't mean to be, but something inside you dies when they laugh at your idea. When they disregard your beliefs, you feel less. These people don't need a front-row seat in your life. They can sit on the balcony as acquaintances but not as close friends.

During the conversation with Telisa, she said she surrounds herself with people who are change agents. These are the types of friends I have in my life. They are powerful but few. What types of people surround you? Are you getting the right type of fuel for your hopes and dreams?

As a reminder the REX Principles we have covered are:

REX Principle #1: Do What Makes YOU Happy

REX Principle #2: Find YOUR Focus

REX Principle #3: Sometimes You Have to Pick Up Poop

REX Principle #4: Begin with the End in Mind

REX Principle #5: Your Inspiration Must Be Bigger than You

REX Principle #6: Never Give Up

REX Principle #7: If You Can Dream It, You Can Achieve It and Please Write It Down

REX Principle #8: Fuel Your Passion with a Network Who Supports You

"You've got
what it takes,
but it will take
everything
you've got."

THOMAS AQUINAS

CHAPTER 9

Execution: Put the Pedal to the Metal

We are finally in line, pushing the car to the starting line. I am sitting behind the wheel of my '79 Malibu with a supercharger in front of me. I hear the whine of the turbos spooling up. I feel the rumble of the car as it shakes, echoing throughout my body. My eyes fixate on the light. My pointer finger raised just a hair, so I can hit the trans-break the moment my foot stomps on the gas pedal. The adrenaline is kicking in and rushing through my veins. You can't compare it to anything. There's nothing like it except perhaps being shot out of a rocket. My heart beats so fast, and my body feels electrified. The team is all there, observing my every move. The guys talk smack, and although I can see their mouths moving, I can't hear them. I watch them gather around the driver in the car next to me, encouraging him. My heart flutters a little. This is my happy place. All of my determination and hard work brought me to this place. My bare hands did this for *me*. A tingle of satisfaction trickles up my spine. I have to stop daydreaming. I must get my mind right before I step on the gas. I need to focus on the race.

Finally, I move up to the starting line, and I am ready to bump in. The engine rumbles so loudly that my teeth rattle. Mothers cover their children's ears as they strain to see what will happen next. The children stare with wide, curious eyes.

The announcer yells, "Mystique has bumped in." Then I hear the whining start. It's the distinctive whine of a supercharger on a motor that sounds like a spinning top on steroids as it revs up and gets ready to go. The rumbling sounds like a row of the fiercest Harley-Davidson motorcycles. But it's not. It's *my* car, Mystique.

Then the announcer says, "This is gonna be a good one," and the second car bumps in. Both are now parallel to each other and in place to begin the race. We have crossed the beam that will activate the stoplight in front of us. The anticipation is deafening. It changes from red to green, and both drivers smash the gas pedal down to the floor. The cars scream down the track, and a gust of hot air flashes over the audience as everyone jumps to their feet, screaming in delight. I can't hear the cheers over the noise of the engine. I can only focus on the finish line, and when I do, I feel free.

I don't know if I won yet. But when I look back, I can see that I crossed the finish line first. "Mark won!" everyone yelled.

All the long hours in the garage turned out to be a success. My legs are shaking. The fleeting feeling of gratification is worth every second of the painstaking work.

I did it. My family is just as excited as I am. Marcus screams, "Daddy; you did it!" Zoe jumps into my arms. "You won, Daddy!"

I smile at my daughter as she hands me a bottle of cold water, and I say, "Let's do that again."

REX PRINCIPLE #9:
EXECUTION: PUT THE PEDAL TO THE METAL

When you experience the joy of seeing a dream come true, like my husband did when he won that race. You never want to let go of that moment. You want to do it again and again.

We all want to find a happy place like the one we shared with Mark in his race car. Sometimes the journey of discovery falls flat. We feel confused. If you are like me. You may enjoy a lot of different things. We all started where you are. Throughout our lives, we will start over and over, again and again. Just remember to focus on one thing for this moment that allows you to enter that state of flow where you experience a feeling of exhilaration that will push you to the next level. Be like Mark, put the pedal to the metal. If you are going to give any goal a try, it's not worth it unless you give 100 percent of yourself. You owe it to yourself to know you did your best.

So, what now? Was this another inspiring little book to tell me that I can do it? You are darned right it is! Now take two more minutes and write down your thoughts.

When you pursue your dream, is it about money or passion? Are you willing to pick up poop?

There is a lot of hard work involved in a business, and I want you to be honest with yourself. If you don't like to sell and your business idea is to sell something, then maybe you should cross that off your list. Being a salesperson is crazy unforgiving hard work or consider getting a partner who does like selling. If you are vacillating on the thought of being a fabulous employee or an enterprising entrepreneur, I highly recommend you read the book *The*

E-Myth by Michael Gerber. If you are the person who is willing to do what it takes, and you don't mind picking up A LOT OF Poop, then WHOO HOO! Go for it!

Here is the next question: What do you love to do so much that you would do it for free?

I have a coworker who makes beautiful wood-workings. It's his labor of love; he only takes on the projects that he wants. The money is more of an afterthought. He told me that he always wants his hobby to be enjoyable and not like a job.

Ask yourself this last question: Do you have a passion for this thing because you want it to make you a lot of money?

Businesses often fail when the passion behind it was just to make a little money. Check out all the "get rich quick" scams you have experienced out there. Making a quick buck is not the goal of Relentless Execution. This book is about finding your purpose, fulfilling your dream, and finishing all the details that will make your dream come true.

- ✓ Find your purpose – take the time to learn why your life is significant.

- ✓ Fulfill your dream – once you know your "why," you will start envisioning "what" you can do next.

- ✓ Finish the details – this is about Execution. You must finish what you start to experience the success that you desire.

When something becomes a fire in your belly, it's hard to quit or even retire because it fills your soul with pride and gratification. The inspiration that cultivates inside of you somehow persuades you to keep going. When you are focused, it is easy to see where you are going, and picking up poop along the way isn't so bad because you know you have an exact destination. Then you can do whatever you set your mind to do.

If you want to write a book, do it. Start today. Write a title. Write an outline. Draft a chapter. **Do** something. Sometimes dreams are like shoes; you need to try them on to see which one is the right fit. *Once you find the fit, the focus, and the fuel, nothing is impossible for you.*

I forgot to mention that you may have fervor for something that may not be a moneymaker, and that's OK. Do what makes YOU happy!

Want to do better? This is it. Before we can be more, we must be able to see what more looks like to us. You have your own stories of how you created something from nothing—or how you finished a project that kept you up all night, and you never thought it would be done—and then one day it was finished. Look back on that moment mentally and remember your sense of accomplishment.

What dream has you fixated on the finished product? Are you ready for your next all-nighter? It's time to stop talking about your dreams and time to start doing them. Let's put the pedal to the metal!

As a reminder the REX Principles we have covered are:

REX Principle #1: Do What Makes YOU Happy

REX Principle #2: Find YOUR Focus

REX Principle #3: Sometimes You Have to Pick Up Poop

REX Principle #4: Begin with the End in Mind

REX Principle #5: Your Inspiration Must Be Bigger than You

REX Principle #6: Never Give Up

REX Principle #7: If You Can Dream It, You Can Achieve It and Please Write It Down

REX Principle #8: Fuel Your Passion with a Network Who Supports You

REX Principle #9: Execution: Put the Pedal to the Metal

"The two most important days in your life are the day you are born and the day you find out why."

MARK TWAIN

CHAPTER 10

Get Your Vision Checked

The morning felt crisp and perfect for a great run. I trained hard for the last few weeks, and this was my moment. Bang, I launched out of the starting blocks.

"Lean forward, keep your form, and pace yourself," were the words from my coach running through my head. The first 300 yards zoomed by. I was in third place. My breathing was steady, and my legs felt good. I thought to myself that my extra training had paid off with dividends. I had a real shot at first place. Then my lungs betrayed me, and I couldn't breathe. I panted, trying to get enough air in my body. I lost my form. I was falling behind, now, in third place. I had to refocus on my training, I knew better. Then I made the worst mistake, I looked back and saw that I was now, in fourth place. I could see the finish line. Adrenaline kicked in, I pumped my arms and legs with ferocity, and I crossed the finish line firmly in fourth place.

Who remembers the girl that came in fourth? No one remembers. But I am that girl, and I recall every agonizing step I took to earn fourth place.

After the race ended, I went to talk to the coach to discuss what happened. The first 300 yards zoomed by. Then I hit "the wall" at the last 100 yards. If you've never run a race, I will describe "the wall" like this. You are running along, minding your own business, then all-of-a sudden this proverbial hand smacks the hell out of you. Everything burns and you can't breathe. Your body feels heavy and that feeling doesn't stop until the race is over. Then you turn the corner and you see the finish line. The moment you SEE the finish line your behavior changes.

Seeing the finish line works. (*Begin with the end in mind*) Visualizing your success before it happens gives you an inner inspiration that will propel you forward if you are struggling to find your focus. Sight is a function of the eyes, but vision comes from the heart. Vision sees what things could be. You need your dream to evolve into an image. Your mind will allow you to see yourself in the boardroom with the VP placard on your door. It will enable you to picture your book's cover, and it will help you see your employees working in your business. Vision invites you to smell the cakes cooking in your bakery. It will allow you to see yourself vacationing on that island you have been dreaming about. Vision sees the future from the present. When you have a clear idea, you stop trying to do everything. You have focus.

How do we stay motivated when we can't see the finish line yet? When I ran the 400-meter dash, I learned to pace myself early in the race. The entire race is a sprint. The race gets harder as you get closer to the finish line when you must plan for the moment you turn the corner at 300 meters and catch that initial glimpse of the finish line. It's about visualizing the entire race. You see yourself crossing the finish line. You know how your body will react when you hit your body's limits. You envision yourself kicking harder, pushing through the pain.

Let's talk about the actual practice of visualization for just a moment.

REX PRINCIPLE #10:
GET YOUR VISION CHECKED

Princess Gabriele Oettingen is known in academia for her work in psychology on visualization and how it impacts cognition, emotion, and behavior. She is credited for being a thought leader on the subject and claims that visualization and action are intimately connected. In her book Rethinking Positive Thinking, she dives into the science of human motivation to reveal why the conventional wisdom of dreaming and thinking positive alone falls short of success for many people. The premise states that visualizing actions literally changes how our brain networks are organized, creating more connections among different regions. It stimulates various regions of the brain that we use to perform more effectively. Many famous athletes use visualization to help them improve their performance.

In a 1997 interview, Jim Carrey talked about the effectiveness of visualization with famous talk show host, Oprah Winfrey. During the interview he describes how he experienced visualization. He shares how he would imagine directors meeting and talking to him about how much they liked his work. He even tells her about the check he wrote himself for $10 Million dollars dated Thanksgiving 1995, three years in the future. He carried the check in his wallet and laughs in the interview at how the check deteriorated over time as he kept working smaller jobs. Jim goes on to share that right around thanksgiving of 1995 he was cast in the movie Dumb and Dumber, and you guessed it, he would finally earn that $10 million dollars.

This is your opportunity to visualize exactly what you dream of doing. If you do not know what you want to do that's ok. Start by thinking about these things.

1. *How do you spend your time?*

2. *What do you enjoy doing?*

3. *Am I willing to do this as my work?*

The point of this is to envision what you truly want to **do**. *When you can see where you are going, you can be fully engaged on the journey to get there.*

A few years ago, I asked my husband how he likes his career as a heavy-repair technician.

He said, "It's basically 'Groundhogs Day' for me every day."

"Yuck! That sucks," I said.

He replied, "Yes, but I enjoy doing things with my hands, so I don't mind it. And when I am at work, I can think about things I want to create later for my racecar."

My husband uses his career to garner ideas for his hobby. Mark is amazing, even on the days when I don't like him that much. He can create something out of nothing without much effort—his mind designs solutions to problems that prevent him from enjoying his favorite pastime.

Sometimes my husband feels frustrated because people don't believe that he creates his own special tools. People can't see his vision. He works tirelessly on his pet project. His idea of success is different than my vision of success. (This is an educational nugget right here.)

Mark's vision of success is to have a good-paying job and retire well with enough money to fund his life and hobbies. He focuses on the end game and executes with precision.

What's your vision? Do you love helping people? Then find a way to volunteer often or change your career.

About changing your career…

I want to mention this. Sometimes we work in jobs that don't excite us, leading us to live a life that lacks fulfillment. Relentless Execution is about doing what you need to do to live a fulfilled life. If you don't like being an engineer, then you don't have to keep doing it. You **can** change your career. When you are focused and not willing to live an unfulfilled life, you will do whatever it takes to execute your dreams.

- My sister, Nicole, did it. She worked as a civil engineer for about 12 years. After the birth of her daughter, she found her work less fulfilling. After some thought, she decided to change. Nicole went back to school and became a math teacher. Now, she feels like she found her calling and she is completely satisfied as an educator.

- My other sister pivoted into a new career, as well. Danielle was a math teacher. She discovered that she preferred helping people solve life issues, so she went back to school, became a counselor, and started her own counseling practice. She feels her purpose is to support young ladies as they navigate adulthood and life.

- Daniel, my brother, switched his Corporate Career for an engaging career as an investigator for the City of Detroit.

- My mother went from being a Librarian to being a Teacher. My father was a Barber who ended up being a Counselor.

- I want to introduce you to one last person: my mother-in-law, Marion. She was a retired nurse who was still in school when she was 80. I would tease her and ask her what she was going to do with another degree. She said, "It's never too late to do something good." She was going to help people.

I want you to know that you can do anything you put your mind to, and as my mother-in-law said, *it's never too late to do something good.*

You were born to do something special. Once you understand your gift, you will never have a job. Every morning, you wake up excited to go to work because your fuel is your passion, like George at Wolverine Harley-Davidson or Telisa at American Family Insurance from earlier in the book. Their focus, passion and action, guided them to the fulfillment of their dreams.

You may want that "boss" placard on your office door. I give you permission to be into titles. If you want a big title, that is OK. You can have that title, but like Amy and every other person in this book, you must be willing to work hard; and you will pick up some poop along the way.

Finally, you may be like Mark, who is happy with his career and finds his flow in his hobby. No one said you must do some major thing. I am suggesting that you have something that adds meaning to your life. I would even propose to you that your passion projects can impact lives in ways that you may never imagine.

Visualize yourself as what you desire to be.

I watched a lot of basketball during the Michael Jordan era and there is nothing like watching a buzzer shot like the one that he got in a final game against the Cleveland Cavaliers when he made a lay-up with 3 seconds left on the clock to clinch the game winning points. I am certain Michael Jordan didn't imagine that he would be up against this particular situation when it happened, but he prepared himself to the best at his craft. Here is my point. Whatever your craft may be, prepare yourself to be the best so that you are ready to perform in any situation. You may be a poet like Amanda Gorman, or a gardener like Alan Titchmarsh the world famous English Gardener. Whatever you do, be the best you can be at doing it. *Visualize yourself as what you desire to be.*

There will be many days when you feel worn down. Tears may stream down your cheeks but keep going until you see the finish line. No one cares if you finish first in this race called life. Give these moments your absolute best. Visualize what you want to do. Push through the self-doubts and fears. Encourage yourself with each small step forward. Discover more about yourself and then get better at being you and then persist until you succeed.

*Dream *Write *Plan *Act

As a reminder the REX Principles we have covered are:

REX Principle #1: Do What Makes YOU Happy

REX Principle #2: Find YOUR Focus

REX Principle #3: Sometimes You Have to Pick Up Poop

REX Principle #4: Begin with the End in Mind

REX Principle #5: Your Inspiration Must Be Bigger than You

REX Principle #6: Never Give Up

REX Principle #7: If You Can Dream It, You Can Achieve It and Please Write it Down

REX Principle #8: Fuel Your Passion with a Network Who Supports You

REX Principle #9: Execution: Put the Pedal to the Metal

REX Principle #10: Get Your Vision Checked

"*Dare to Dream,
but please
also do.
For Dreamers
are many,
but doers
are few*"

BRAD MONTAGUE

Finding your "It."

Have you ever walked into a kitchen and picked up a tool that looks like it belongs in the garage instead? My husband doesn't understand why I use a tenderizer mallet. He thought a tenderizer was only a spice. When I pulled out a tool that looked like a mallet, he was totally confused. He didn't understand the purpose of a mallet in the kitchen until he bit into the steak I prepared for dinner. The delicate chew and soft bite made him smile in delight as he enjoyed the suppleness of the steak. Many of us are like that tenderizer mallet. We were created to do something special but often we don't have a clear understanding around how our lives can have an impact on the world much like that tenderizer mallet in the kitchen.

You were created to do something special. You have a purpose. Some would call it a "why". The dash in between the day you were born and the day you die is the most important part of your life. It's during the dash that you changed the future or rewrote the ending to someone's life story. Sometimes you can't see exactly how you fit into the grand plan. But your uniqueness is distinctly important. You are designed intricately like the clumsy bee who pollinates a desolate field without knowing that he has created a work of art as he works with singular focus to simply build a comfortable home. Your life represents a key link in a chain reaction of pivotal events that can alter the very world we live in today and the unspoken truth is that we may not know the impact you will make until after you are gone. A host of people unknowingly look forward to seeing your face when you go to your art class or when you stop to get coffee on your commute to work. Your passions have people behind them. When you find your "it"—the "it" I talked about at the beginning of this book, you function on a higher level where you experience your true enlightened self. This is when you overcome your own weaknesses in life, find peace and make an indelible mark on the lives of others.

A study in an issue of the Personality and Social Psychology Bulletin shows that about 90% of adults have deep regrets about their lives. I want you to be in the 10% that lives life without regrets. As I end this book, I want you to think about this question:

- What are you willing to do today to ensure that you live your life to the fullest without regrets?

  Today, I will _____

  _____

  _____

  _____

  _____.

> *"Dare to Dream, but please also do.*
> *For Dreamers are many, but doers are few."*
>
> BRAD MONTAGUE

This is the end of the book—but not the end of our journey together. These authors share messages of encouragement and provide insightful details to help you throughout your quest to personal fulfillment.

Recommended Reading List

As a Man Thinketh by James Allen

Start with Why by Simon Sinek

Range by David Epstein

Everything is Figureoutable by Marie Forleo

The E-Myth by Michel Gerber

The Gig Economy by Diane Mulcahy

Leapfrog by Nathalie Molina Nino

Rethinking Positive Thinking by Gabrielle Oettingen

Make Your Bed by Admiral William H. McRaven

Boss Up! by Lindsay Teague Moreno

The Four Agreements by Don Miguel Ruiz

The Energy Bus by Jon Gordon

Yolanda Spearman is a native of Detroit, Michigan where she grew up in a close-knit family. She is the proud mother of two children, Zoe and Marcus, and the wife of Mark, of whom you hear a lot about in her writings.

Living an adventurous life, Yolanda served as a missionary in West Africa, studied Art and Humanities in Paris, France and researched the shoe industry on an enthralling entrepreneurial trip to China.

Yolanda's careers in the Detroit Public School System, Ford Motor Company and Harley-Davidson Financial Services developed her business acumen and leadership abilities. Throughout these endeavors Yolanda's unwavering optimism propelled her forward in her careers and always allowed her the opportunity to speak into people's lives. It is not uncommon to catch her coaching even during her downtime.

She spends her spare time investing, gardening, biking, ballroom dancing, and working as a very successful Voiceover Talent.

This short biography is only a snapshot of Yolanda's multitude of adventures throughout her travels and the mini-careers she didn't mention.

*Meet her at **WillYouBeRelentless.Com***

Made in the USA
Monee, IL
23 April 2021

66561398R00073